AIR WAR ARCHIVE

DORNIER Do 17

THE LUFTWAFFE'S 'FLYING PENCIL'

T0286048

DORNIER Do 17
THE LUFTWAFFE'S 'FLYING PENCIL'

RARE LUFTWAFFE PHOTOGRAPHS FROM WARTIME COLLECTIONS

CHRIS GOSS

FRONTLINE
BOOKS

DORNIER Do 17
The Luftwaffe's 'Flying Pencil'

This edition published in 2018 by Frontline Books,
an imprint of Pen & Sword Books Ltd,
47 Church Street, Barnsley, S. Yorkshire, S70 2AS

ISBN: 978-1-84832-471-8

CIP data records for this title are available from the British Library.

Pen & Sword Books Limited incorporates the imprints of Atlas, Archaeology, Aviation, Discovery, Family History, Fiction, History, Maritime, Military, Military Classics, Politics, Select, Transport, True Crime, Air World, Frontline Publishing, Leo Cooper, Remember When, Seaforth Publishing, The Praetorian Press, Wharncliffe Local History, Wharncliffe Transport, Wharncliffe True Crime and White Owl.

For more information on our books, please visit
www.frontline-books.com, email info@frontline-books.com
or write to us at the above address.

Typeset by Aura Technology and Software Services, India
Printed and bound by CPI Group (UK) Ltd, Croydon, CR0 4YY

Typeset in 9.5/12pt Avenir

CONTENTS

V

ACKNOWLEDGEMENTS

I would like to thank the following for their assistance in compiling this book: Bernd Rauchbach, Tim Oliver, Peter Cornwell and the late Dr Alfred Price.

INTRODUCTION

The Dornier Do 17 Fliegender Bleistift (Flying Pencil) has been linked with the rise of Hitler, regularly being seen flying over the pre-Second World War Nuremberg rallies. However, despite its radical design and technologically superior construction, by the summer of 1941, it was all but obsolete.

EARLY DEVELOPMENT

In October 1935, Dornier revealed its Do 17 V1, a twin-engined commercial transport aircraft that had first flown in on 23 November 1934 and was capable of carrying six passengers at relatively high speed. In the years that followed, it was modified and in July 1937, the Do 17 V8 participated in the International Military Aircraft Competition at Zürich, where it won the 'Circuit of the Alps' and showed that contemporary fighters might have difficulty in catching it.

Deutsche Lufthansa (DLH) had placed a requirement for a high-speed mail plane, capable of carrying six passengers, for use on its European express service. The Do 17's aerodynamic design together with the twin liquid-cooled BMW VI engines – the most powerful aero engines available in Germany at that time – met this requirement but also enabled it to achieve speeds nearly 60mph superior to other aircraft entering service with the embryonic Luftwaffe.

Following the first flight of the Do 17 V1, identical versions V2 and V3 were passed to DLH in early 1935. The airline was pleased with the speed and mail carrying potential but quickly concluded that the design was impractical from a passenger viewpoint with two tiny cabins, one for two passengers behind the flight deck and

another for four behind the wing. DLH therefore rejected the aircraft.

The saviour of the Do 17 was now former Dornier employee Flugkapitän Robert Untucht, who was working for DLH as its liaison between the airline and Reichsluftfahrtministerium (RLM). He had the opportunity to fly one of the prototypes and was impressed by the handling qualities and performance, and suggested that with modifications, the aircraft could be a good bomber. He persuaded Dornier and the RLM that this was possible and after subsequent flights, Dornier was instructed to produce Do 17 V4, which differed in that the passenger carrying aspects, such as the portholes, were removed and the single fin replaced by a twin fin. Removal of the forward passenger compartment allowed an expansion of the flight deck and the fitting of a bomb bay. Two more prototypes were built: V5 was identical to V4, whilst V6 was powered by Hispano-Suiza engines, giving it a maximum speed of over 240mph. This speed meant that V6 was faster than many fighters of other nations, which meant that defensive armament was superfluous. Nevertheless, as well as a partly glazed nose, V7 included a fuselage-mounted blister behind the cockpit and was armed with a single 7.9mm machine gun.

V8, the showpiece at Zürich, was retained by Dornier as a development aircraft but V9 was the shape of things to come. Essentially, the nose length was reduced, the glazed nose increased, the fuselage-mounted blister refined and the vertical tail surfaces enlarged. Furthermore, V9 was fitted out as a military aircraft; for all intents and purposes, V9 was identical to the full production Do 17 E (bomber) and F (reconnaissance) variants, which in early 1936 now started to roll off the production line. There was a final prototype – the V10 variant, which was a flying test bed for the BMW VI engine. After this, the Do 17 began to be mass produced.

MASS PRODUCTION –
THE E & F VARIANTS

The Do 17 E-1 (bomber) and Do 17 F-1 (reconnaissance) versions were produced at Dornier's factories at Allmansweiler, Löwenthal and Manzell. Both variants were essentially the same, the latter having no bomb sight (and no noticeable bulge underneath the nose) and no internal bomb racks. Instead, the F-1 had additional fuel tanks and two vertical cameras in the bomb bay. Armament wise, both aircraft types had the rear-firing MG 15 in the gondola and later a second MG 15 was fitted to fire downwards through the bomb bay. The Do 17 E-1 could carry a 1,100lb bomb load, which could rise to 1,650lbs on shorter range missions.

Another success of the production line was Dornier's decision to break the airframe down into major components, which allowed sub-contractorisation and ease of component replacement. This was soon adopted by other aircraft manufacturers but this allowed the Do 17 to be delivered to the Luftwaffe by early 1937.

The first units to convert to the Do 17 E-1 were I Gruppe/Kampfgeschwader 153 (I/KG 153) at Merseburg and I/KG 155 at Giebelstadt. Simultaneously, Aufklärungsgruppe (Fern)122 ((F)/122) at Prenzlau began converting to the Do 17 F-1. The remaining Gruppen of KG 153 and KG 155 converted throughout 1937, with KG 255 forming at Landsberg in the spring of 1937.

With this rapid expansion of Do 17-equipped units came the opportunity to test the aircraft in combat. In spring 1938, elements of (F)/122

(soon to be re-designated (F)/22) were sent to Spain to form A/88. Its performance impressed High Command, the aircraft being virtually immune to fighter attacks, and the Do 17 F-1 then replaced the Heinkel 70 in Spain as well as re-equipping all long-range reconnaissance units in Germany. In August 1938, the Legion Condor Do 17s, known affectionately as Bacalaos (Spanish for cod), were transferred to the Spanish Nationalist Grupo 8-G-27 at La Cenia and continued to serve with this unit for a number of years. However, as the Spanish Civil War had escalated, more modern fighter aircraft, specifically of Soviet manufacture, proved capable of intercepting the Do 17 E-1 and F-1, which gave an impetus to improve the Do 17

NEXT GENERATION –
THE M AND P VARIANTS

With the Do 17 E and F in full production, Dornier now began looking at improving the basic design. The Do 17 V8 had been re-engined with Daimler-Benz DB 600A liquid-cooled engines and improved airscrew designs and re-designated the Do 17M V1. As impressive as its performance was, the decision was made that the DB 600 engine would be for fighter aircraft use only, forcing Dornier to consider the air-cooled radial Bramo Fafnir 323 A-1 engine. The conversion from liquid-cooled to air-cooled engines was relatively easy and in 1938, the Do 17 E and F started to be replaced by the Do 17 M (bomber) and P (reconnaissance) variants, but in the search for increased range, the Do 17 P was later powered by the BMW 132 N radial engine. As a result of the Spanish 'proving ground', armament was increased by a forward-mounted MG 15, fired by the pilot or observers, whilst the bomb bay in the Do 17 M was stretched, increasing the payload to 2,205lbs.

In 1938, the two new variants began to replace the older variants in Spain as well as Germany and by late summer, in the region of 480 Do 17s of all variants were in service. However, by then, Dornier was looking at the next generation of Do 17, even though the Do 17 M and P continued to be operated by reconnaissance units for another three years.

THE ULTIMATE VARIANT – THE DO 17 Z

As a result of Spain, Dornier comprehensively redesigned the forward fuselage. The cockpit roof was raised and completely glazed whilst the nose was similarly glazed in addition to the lower part of the cockpit area being bulged and extended back towards the leading edge, at the rear of which was an MG 15 machine gun. This design was used on the Do 17 S, which had liquid-cooled DB 600G engines, but only three examples of this aircraft were produced and the Luftwaffe preferred subsequent models. Next came the DB 600A powered Do 17 U, a five-seat pathfinder version of which fifteen were produced. However, by now the decree that DB 600 engines would be reserved for fighters had resulted in the modified airframe being powered by Bramo Fafnir 323A engines and the ultimate version – the Do 17 Z.

The Do 17 Z-1 was essentially the same as the M-1, apart from the forward fuselage, and despite the relatively un-aerodynamic forward fuselage, performance remained unchanged. However, when a fourth crew member, increased defensive armament and a 2,205lb bomb load were added, the Z-1 was underpowered. The answer was to halve the bomb load or re-engine. The Do 17 Z-2, therefore, was fitted with the Bramo Fafnir 323P engine but it still meant that with a full bomb load, its operational radius was just over 200 miles. The Do 17 Z-3 had a reduced bomb load and installation of automatic cameras, whilst the latter two variants were the Do 17 Z-4 dual control trainer and the Do 17 Z-5 fitted with additional floatation aids and life-saving equipment for maritime operations.

However, the Do 17's Achilles Heel still remained its small bomb load and limited range, thus it soon became sidelined by the Heinkel 111's bigger bomb load and the Junkers 88's speed and range. By the end of 1939, production was coming to an end and that came in the summer of 1940, after which some 500 Do 17 Z-1 and Z-2 and twenty-two Z-3 aircraft had been built. Those Do 17 units that fought in the Battle of France and the Battle of Britain now began to convert to the Junkers 88 so that by the invasion of Russia on June 22

1941, KG 2 was the sole Do 17 Z Geschwader and a few months later, it too converted to the Do 217, leaving just III/KG 3 as the only Do 17-equipped bomber Gruppe, which then began converting to the Junkers 88 in December 1941. From that date onwards, the Do 17 was used for minor or secondary roles, particularly in communications. It did participate on operations in the glider tug role – Do 17s of Luftlandegeschwader 1 participated in supply and evacuation of the German 17th Army at Kuban from February to October 1943, and it was still being used by Schleppgruppen 1 and 2 in early 1945.

THE DO 17 NIGHT FIGHTER

There were two versions of the Do 17 night fighter – the Z-7 Kauz I and the Z-10 Kauz II, Kauz meaning screech owl. The glazed nose was removed from a Do 17 Z-3 and replaced by the nose from a Junkers 88 C fighter, the Dornier Do 17 now being designated the Do 17 Z-7. The armament was three 7.9mm machine guns and one 20mm cannon but this was found to be unsatisfactory and an entirely new nose was designed, which increased the armament to four machine guns and two cannon. In the tip of the nose was an infra-red spotlight called Spanner Anlage, which was later replaced by first-generation radar. This was now designated the Do 17 Z-10.

Only one Do 17 Z-7 and nine Do 17 Z-10s were produced and first entered service with 5/Nachtjagdgeschwader 1 (5/NJG 1) in early summer of 1940. Limited successes ensued and the aircraft was used extensively on intruder missions over the UK but, like its bomber and reconnaissance brethren, was found to be inferior to the Junkers 88. In mid-1941, the Dornier Do 17 Z-10 was reinforced by a number of Dornier Do 215B-5 night fighters of 4/NJG 1 but both types were withdrawn from service by mid-1941 when more Junkers 88 C night fighters became available.

OTHER NATIONS & EXPORT VARIANTS

Having been impressed by the Dornier Do 17 V8 at Zürich, Yugoslavia placed an immediate order for twenty aircraft as well as seeking permission to manufacture the aircraft under licence. Yugoslavia wanted the Dornier Do 17, designated the Do 17 K, to be powered by Gnome-Rhône 14N 1/2 engines, made under licence just outside Belgrade, and supplied the engines to Dornier who then delivered a mix of twenty bomber and reconnaissance variants in October 1937. Construction of the Do 17 K was at Kraljevo with deliveries commencing in early 1940. By the time the Germans attacked Yugoslavia on 6 April 1941, there were in the region of sixty Do 17 Ks, which instantly became a target for the Luftwaffe. Twenty-six were destroyed in the initial assault and those that survived were quickly shot down, badly damaged or captured. The final losses were estimated as four lost in combat, forty-five destroyed on the ground, seven fled to Greece, two fled to the Soviet Union and one defected with its crew. Of the seven that went to Greece, two ended up with the RAF in Egypt whilst those that were left in Yugoslavia were handed over to the Croatian Air Force the following year to supplement a number of Dornier Do 17 Es given to them by the Luftwaffe where, operating from Zagreb and Banja Luka, they carried out anti-partisan missions.

When Croatian volunteers were called to fight the Soviet Union, in addition to a fighter unit, Lieutenant Colonel Vjekoslav Vicevic formed a bomber unit, officially designated 10 (kroat.)/KG 3. By the end of July 1941, this unit was being trained at Grosse Kampffliegerschule 3 at Greifswald. They were equipped with the Do 17 Z and arrived at Vitebsk in October 1941,

returning to Zagreb in July 1942 to reform as 15 (Kroatisch)/KG 53. They then returned to the Eastern Front but the unit returned to Croatia in December 1942, where it was later understood to have been employed on anti-partisan missions.

The Bulgarian Air Force operated eleven Do 17 M-1s and P-1s in 1940 and was later given fifteen captured Yugoslav Do 17Ks; they received another six Do 17s later in the war. The Royal Romanian Air Force also received ten Do 17 Ms.

The only other nation to use the Do 17 was Finland, which, in January 1942, was given fifteen Do 17 Zs, made up of four Do 17 Z-1s, two Z-2s and nine Z-3s. They were assigned to PLeLv 46, latterly PLeLv 43 and 44, and began day and night operations in April 1942, the first loss occurring on 23 May 1942. By July 1944, just seven were left, the survivors being scrapped from 1947 to 1952.

SURVIVORS

Until June 2013, no complete Dornier Do 17 existed. However, the RAF Museum has recently recovered the remains of a Do 17 Z, believed to be from 7/KG 3, having been shot down on 26 August 1940 over the English Channel. It is essentially complete, albeit the fuselage, wing section and engines being separate, and is currently undergoing restoration at the RAF Museum at Cosford, near Wolverhampton. Restoration, which involves soaking the aircraft with fresh water and citric acid, will take up to two years to complete, after which it will be displayed as it is at the RAF Museum at Hendon in London.

GLOSSARY AND ABBREVIATIONS

AA	Anti-aircraft
Adj	Adjutant
Aufklärungsgruppe	Reconnaissance wing
Aufklärungsstaffel	Reconnaissance squadron
Bordfunker (BF)	Radio operator
Beobachter (BO or B)	Observer
Bordmechaniker (BM)	Flight engineer
Bordschütze (BS)	Air gunner
Deutsches Kreuz in Gold (DKiG)	German Cross in Gold award
Do	Dornier
Ehrenpokal (Pokal)	Goblet of Honour; awarded for outstanding achievements in the air war
Eisernes Kreuz (EK)	Iron Cross (awarded in First and Second Class)
Ergänzungs (Erg)	Training
Fahnenjunker (Fhr)	Flight officer
Feindflug	Operational flight
Feldwebel (Fw)	Flight sergeant
Fern	Long range
Flak	Anti-aircraft
Flieger (Flg)	Aircraftman
Fliegerführer Atlantik	Air Commander for the Atlantic region
Flugzeugführer (F)	Pilot
Flugzeugführerschule	Pilot school
Frontflugspange	Mission Clasp – awarded for operational flights
Führer	Leader
Gefreiter (Gefr)	Leading aircraftman
Generalfeldmarschall	Air Chief Marshal
Geschwader (Gesch)	Group consisting three Gruppen commanded by a Geschwaderkommodore (Gesch Komm)
Gruppe (Gr)	Wing comprising three Staffeln, commanded by a Gruppenkommandeur (Gr Kdr). The Gruppe number is denoted by Roman numerals (e.g. II)

Hauptmann (Hptm)	Flight Lieutenant/Captain
He	Heinkel
Ia	Operations officer
Jabo	Fighter bomber
Ju	Junkers
Kampfgeschwader (KG)	Bomber group
Kampfgeschwader zur besonderen Verwendung (KGzbV)	Normal designation for a transport unit
Kampfgruppe	Brigade group
Kette	Three aircraft tactical formation similar to RAF vic
Kriegsmarine	German navy
Küstenfliegergruppe	Coast reconnaissance and naval support group
Lehrgeschwader (LG)	Technical development flying group
Leutnant (Lt)	Pilot officer/2nd lieutenant
Luftflotte	Air Fleet
Major (Maj)	Squadron leader/major
Me	Messerschmitt (used by RAF)
Nachtjagdgeschwader (NJG)	Night fighter group
Nachtrichtenoffizier (NO)	Communications officer
Oberfeldwebel (Ofw)	Warrant officer
Obergefreiter (Ogefr)	Senior aircraftman/corporal
Oberleutnant (Oblt)	Flying officer/1st lieutenant
Oberst	Group captain/colonel
Oberstleutnant (Obstlt)	Wing commander/lieutenant colonel
Reichsluftfahrtministerium (RLM)	Germany Air Ministry
Reichsmarschall	Marshal of the Air Force
Ritterkreuz (RK)	Knight's Cross
Ritterkreuz mit Eichenlaub (EL)	Knight's Cross with Oakleaves
Rotte	Two aircraft tactical formation; two Rotten made a Schwarm; commanded by a Rottenführer
Rottenflieger	Wingman
Schlacht (S)	Ground attack
Schwarm	Four aircraft tactical formation commanded by a Schwarm Führer
Seenotflugkommando	Air sea rescue detachment
Sonderführer (Sd Fhr)	Rank usually given to war reporters
Sonderstaffel	Special Staffel
Stab	Staff or HQ; formation in which the Gruppenkommandeur and Geschwaderkommodore flew
Stabsfeldwebel (Stfw)	Senior warrant officer
Staffel (St)	Squadron (12 aircraft); commanded by a Staffelkapitän (St Kap). Staffel number denoted by Arabic numerals (e.g. 2)
Staffelkapitän (Staka)	Squadron commander
Technischer Offizier (TO)	Technical officer
Unteroffizier (Uffz)	Sergeant
Werk Nummer (Wk Nr)	Serial number
Zerstörer (Z)	Destroyer/heavy fighter
Zerstörergeschwader (ZG)	Heavy fighter group
Zur See	Naval rank, i.e. Leutnant zur See (Lt zS)

Part I
EARLY DEVELOPMENT AND PRE-WAR DEPLOYMENT

A Dornier Do 17 M of I/KG 252. This unit was formed at Cottbus, in Brandenburg, on 1 November 1938, and on 1 May 1939 was re-designated I/KG 2. The unit carried diagonal nosebands (white for I Gruppe, red for II Gruppe and yellow for III Gruppe) on its Do 17 Ms, Do 17 Zs and ultimately on its Do 217s. Note the bomb sight housing, which clearly identifies this as an M (bomber) as opposed to P (reconnaissance).

An earlier variant – a Do 17 E of 4/KG 155. The number 53 indicates KG 155; 2 indicates II Gruppe; and 4 indicates 4 Staffel. The letter C is the individual aircraft code. Formed at Ansbach-Neukirchen, Bavaria on 1 April 1936, on 1 February 1938 it was re-designated II/KG 158 and after that became II/KG 77. The aircraft D-OQAO in the background is a Focke-Wulf Fw 58.

Spain saw many Luftwaffe aircraft being used. In this case, these Do 17 Ps are from the reconnaissance unit A/88. Note the devil's head badge on the cowling of the furthest aircraft; this badge was also seen on the nose of A/88's Dornier Do 17 Fs.

What appears to be a line-up of Dornier Do 17 Es. All are in wartime camouflage so they could be from an unknown training unit as by the outbreak of war, Do 17 Es had been replaced by Do 17 Ms, which themselves were being replaced by Do 17 Zs.

A very new Dornier Do 17 P of 3(F)/123. This unit was formed on 1 November 1938 at Würzburg, northern Bavaria, where this photograph was taken.

A Do 17 of 3(F)/123 getting airborne from Würzburg. Note the pre-war markings and camouflage on the aircraft in the background.

This Dornier Do 17 P is a bit of an enigma. What appears to be '9K' ahead of the cross would indicate Kampfgeschwader 51 (formerly KG 255), but this unit had exchanged its Do 17 Es for Heinkel He IIIs.

Many early Dornier Do 17s carried individual names. This Do 17 P is from 1(F)/120, which was formed on 11 November 1938 in Neuhausen, north-east Germany. Again, the absence of a bulge under the nose proves this to be a reconnaissance aircraft.

Part II
THE ATTACK
ON POLAND

Refuelling a Dornier Do 17 Z of 7/KG 3 at Heiligenbeil, eastern Germany, in September 1940. KG 3 had only changed from its pre-war fuselage markings such as 32+N37 to the more recongisable 5K+BR at the end of July 1939.

Opposite above: An unidentified crew from 7/KG 3 photographed at Heilingenbeil on 15 September 1939. III KG/3 adopted Aces as their badge, with Clubs for 7 Staffel, Spades for 8 Staffel and Hearts for 9 Staffel.

Opposite below: A 5K+BR of 7/KG 3, photographed in September 1939.

Taken on or about 10 September 1939 at Heiligenbeil, right to left: Hauptmann Ernst Freiherr von Bibra (possibly Staffelkapitän of 7/KG 3), Oberleutnant Dietrich Marwitz, Feldwebel Markau, Feldwebel Hoffmann and Unteroffizier Hans Fedder. Von Marwitz would be awarded the Ritterkreuz, Ehrenpokal and Deutsches Kreuz in Gold but was killed on 15 February 1943 commanding III/KG 51. Marwitz would be killed in action on 27 October 1940 commanding 8/KG 30.

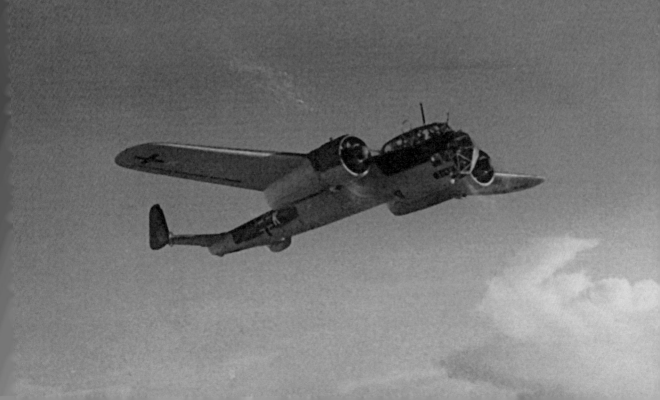

Aircraft of 7/KG 3 photographed in September 1939.
As well as Staffel badges, the aircraft also have names;
the nearest has a second name to the rear of the nose
whilst 5K+GR's name cannot be read.

A Dornier Do 17 P of 1(F)/120 after a taxiing accident either at Neuhausen or Heiligenbeil, in September
1939. On the nose is the unit's reindeer head badge.

The nose of A6+AH of 1(F)/120, at Heiligenbeil in September 1939. The inscription reads: 'Vom Himmel hoch da komm ich her / ach wenn ich doch erst unten war' (Here I come from high in the sky, ah but if only I were on the ground just now).

A closer view of the badge of 1(F)/120. Note the aircraft data plate at the bottom of the nose.

A Dornier Do 17 P of 3(H)/10. The Gruppe had the name 'Tannenberg' and the badge was a black cross on a white shield. This unit was formed at Neuhausen on 1 November 1938 and during the Polish Campaign of 1939, supported the 3rd Armee from Wiesenhof.

The exposed and cramped cockpit of a Dornier Do 17 Z. The Luftwaffe airmen include the Flugzeugführer front left, the Beobachter right, and possibly the Bordmechaniker far left, with the photograph being taken by the Bordfunker.

Camouflaging a Dornier Do 17 P, possibly from 4(F)/14. This unit was formed in November 1938, and in the summer of 1939 was operating from Mankendorf, in the Czech Republic.

An aircraft and crew of 7/KG 3, Heiligenbeil, photographed in the summer of 1939. Note that there are no unit badges on the aircraft.

A crewman stands on the wing of a Dornier Do 17 Z from 7/KG 3 at Heiligenbeil in the summer of 1939, giving a good indication of the aircraft's size.

Aircrew with their Dornier Do 17 from 7/KG 3, pictured at Heiligenbeil in Germany in the summer of 1939. Far left is Bordfunker Unteroffizier Willi Lüder, who was shot down and taken prisoner on 15 August 1940 while flying with II/LG 1.

Unteroffizier Elsner's crew, from 7/KG 3, photographed at Heiligenbeil in the summer of 1939.

Ground crew posing on the fuselage of a Dornier Do 17 Z. Note the unit codes cannot be read as it would appear they are in the process of being applied.

Flak damage to a Dornier Do 17 Z of KG 77, photographed in September 1939.

This Dornier Do 17 Z of 9/KG 3 carried the 'Ace of Hearts' badge and the name *Thea*, at Heiligenbeil in September 1939. (Via Tim Oliver)

Dornier Do 17s from 9/KG 3 on a training flight in the autumn of 1939. The leading aircraft appears to be 5K+AT, which would possibly be that flown by the Staffelkapitän. (Via Tim Oliver)

A Dornier Do 17 Z of 9/KG 3 coded 5K+BT, the 'B' in yellow standing for *Blücher*, which is written above it. (Via Tim Oliver)

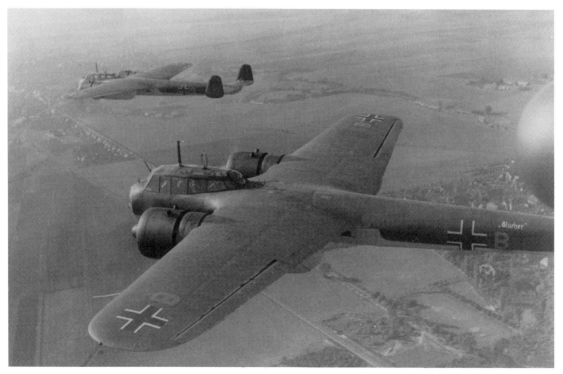

Aircraft 5K+KT carries the 'Ace of Hearts', the name *Traudl*, and again, above the letter 'T' is written something that cannot be deciphered. (Via Tim Oliver)

What appears to be a full Staffel formation flight from 9/KG 3 photographed in the autumn of 1939. (Via Tim Oliver)

On this aircraft from 9/KG 3, the 'Ace of Hearts' is shown as a playing card. (Via Tim Oliver)

This Dornier Do 17 P of 1(F)/120, coded A6+GH, is pictured upon its return to Heiligenbeil in September 1939, after an encounter with a Polish fighter aircraft.

A Dornier Do 17 Z which is believed to be from I/KG 77. Just about visible on the nose is a badge that appears to be a devil riding a bomb. The full code is 3Z+AK.

Part III
WAR IN THE WEST

A pair of brand-new Dornier Do 17 Zs of 9/KG 76. Note the code F1+JT on the furthest aircraft; J would be in yellow, as would the spinners. This unit would become famous for its low-level attacks, particularly that against Kenley on 18 August 1940. At the time this photograph was taken, 9/KG 76 was commanded by Oberleutnant Rudolf Strasser, who would be killed on 19 May 1940.

F1+AM was the aircraft flown by the Staffelkapitän of 4/KG 76, Hauptmann Helmuth von Raven. Von Raven would be awarded the Deutsches Kreuz in Gold on 24 September 1942 whilst with II/KG 51, after which he became Gruppenkommandeur of I/KG 54. He survived the war. At the end of the Battle of France, in June 1940, II/KG 76 disbanded in preparation for conversion to the Junkers Ju 88. Its Dornier Do 17s were dispersed to I and III/KG 76, and in some cases retained their original Staffel badges, which has caused confusion to historians over the years.

F1+GM of 4/KG 76 taxiing out at the start of the Battle of France. Note the fuselage band adopted by KG 76, which differs to the diagonal noseband used by KG 2.

Another new Dornier Do 17 Z, this time F1+AK of 2/KG 76. The letter A would be in red, as would the spinners. The flag and the letter A would indicate this aircraft as being flown by the Staffelkapitän.

At 10.45 hours on 23 November 1939, Flying Officer Cyril Palmer, together with Flying Officer John Kilmartin and Sergeant Frank Soper of 1 Squadron, intercepted and shot down a Dornier Do 17 P, Werk Nummerr 3595, coded F6+FM of 4(F)/122. The aircraft then crash-landed almost intact at Moirement, west of Verdun in north-eastern France, giving the RAF the chance to inspect in some detail the German aircraft, especially the RC 50/30 camera, which is seen here. The camera had been hit by one bullet, which had passed centrally through the camera body without damaging the internal mechanism. Of the crew, Unteroffizier Alfred Röder was captured wounded, whilst Unteroffizier Arno Frankenberger was captured unhurt. Unteroffizier Klaus Ehlers baled out but was killed.

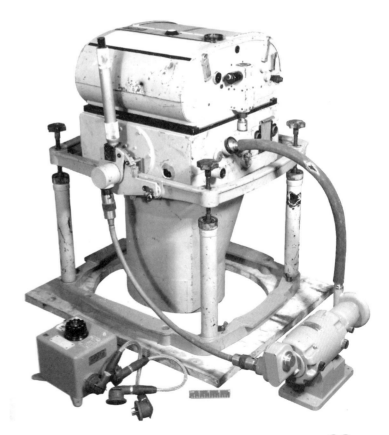

Dornier Do 17 Zs of an unidentified unit pictured practising low-level formation flying. The aircraft furthest from the camera still has factory, as opposed to unit, codes. Both have white spinners.

This Do 17 of 5K+GK, coded 2/KG 3, is pictured here at the start of the Battle of France. It is believed that the badge shows the silhouette of Prussia in black with thee Dornier Do 17s in white superimposed over it. The regular pilot of this aircraft was Leutnant Erich Kunst, who would be brought down by flak off the Norfolk coast on 7 March 1941, and taken prisoner.

Mechanics working on a Dornier Do 17 Z of I/KG 76, in the spring or summer of 1940.

Above and opposite: While on a training flight on 8 April 1940, this Dornier Do 17 P of 3(F)/123 crashed into woodland at Forsthaus Wolfgang, east of Hanau in Germany. The pilot, Oberleutnant Georg Beisiegel, and mechanic, Obergefreiter Johann Schadl, were both killed. Beisiegel was the Gruppe Techischer Offizier and it is assumed that they were carrying out a rectification flight. A memorial to the aircraft and crew still exists at the crash site today.

Photographed during a ceremony forming part of Beisiegel' and Schadl's funeral, the Dornier Do 17 P on the right carries the 3(F)/123 Eiserne Dritte (Iron Third) black hammer and anvil on a yellow shield and the name *Eisbär* (Polar Bear). The significance of the two vertical bars is unknown.

A closer view of the 3(F)/123 badge. This aircraft carries the name *Holzauge* (*Lookout*).

It would appear that this Dornier Do 17 P is from a tactical (Heer or H) as opposed to strategic (Fern or F) unit as the officer on the turret of the Panzer III is Luftwaffe and the aircraft is parked up (with wheel covered) and being worked on by mechanics. The last two letters of the code +JH gives no indication of the unit.

Refuelling a Dornier Do 17 P at its forward airfield, in the spring or summer of 1940.

The reason for the fly-past is not known, unless the older Dornier Do 17 E/Fs are in the process of being replaced by the newer parked-up Do 17 Zs.

A Dornier Do 17 Z believed to be from Kampfgeschwader 76 in action during 1940.

A poignant photograph of a Dornier Do 17 P that force-landed in France - the image was discovered by a German soldier in a French building during the Blitzkrieg in May and June 1940. It is believed that this is the wreckage of a 4(F)/121 aircraft - that coded 7A+KM. This Do 17 P-1 was shot down by Sergeant Jean Doudiès and Sergeant Sonntag of GC II/7 over Luxeuil-les-Bains during reconnaissance of airfields between Remiremont and Montbéliard in north-eastern France, and crash-landed near the railway station at Harol, west of Épinal, at 08.34 hours on 2 March 1940. Unteroffizier Karl-Heinz Jagielki (Flugzeugführer) and Unteroffizier Alfred Matheus (Beobachter) were both killed, whilst Gefreiter Karl Reschke (Bordfunker) baled out and was captured wounded.

An air-to-air shot of a Dornier Do 17 P of 3(F)/123 showing the clean splinter camouflage, which was used by many reconnaissance units up to the summer of 1940.

Above and opposite: One of the first losses of the Battle of France was this Dornier Do 17 Z, coded 5K+CA, of Stab/KG 3. Intercepted by Hurricanes of 1 Squadron (Flight Lieutenant Peter Walker, Flying Officer Mark Brown, Flying Officer John Kilmartin, Flying Officer Paul Richey and Sergeant Frank Soper) during a reconnaissance sortie over Étain-Rouvres, it force-landed at Mont-Saint-Martin, north of Longwy in north-eastern France, at 06.30 hours on 10 May 1940. Oberfeldwebel Hans Schachtebeck (Flieger), Oberfeldwebel Karl Sommer (Beobachter) and Unteroffizier Wilhelm Schmeis (Bordfunker) were all captured, whilst Unteroffizier Rolf Wagner (Bordmechaniker) was killed.

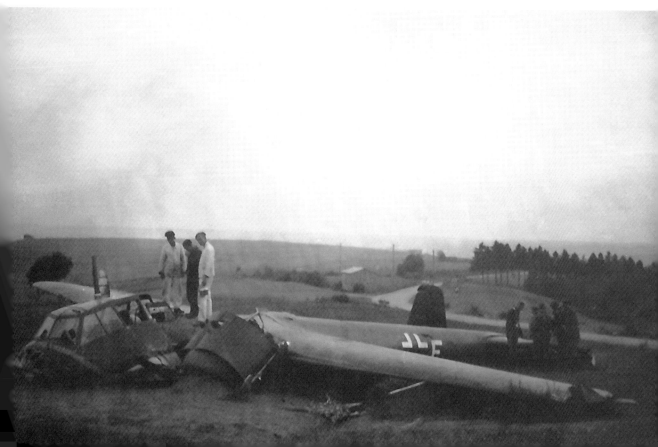

Above and previous spread: One of the most photographed aircraft crashes of the Blitzkrieg in 1940 was that of Dornier Do 17 Z Werk Nummer 6036, coded U5+ER, of 7/KG 2. Damaged by flak, it crash-landed at Ferme Giffaumont, near Izel, at 18.10 hours on 12 May 1940. Feldwebel Willi Klöttschen (Flugzeugführer), Leutnant Dietrich Giesecke (Beobachter), Unteroffizier Paul Tillner (Bordfunker) and Feldwebel Hans Rösl (Bordmechaniker) were all captured wounded, but later repatriated.

Above and below: On 12 May 1940, this Dornier Do 17 Z, Werk Nummer 2550 and coded 5K+BA, was first damaged by flak south-west of Compiègne and then attacked and shot down by Curtis H-75s of GC I/5 flown by Captain Jean Accart and Sergeant Francois Morel. It force-landed at Redu, France, at 10.15 hours. Oberfeldwebel Fritz Schwede (Bordfunker) was wounded, though the remainder of Hauptmann Georgfriedrich Altvater's (Beobachter and Staffelkapitän) crew was unhurt.

An unidentified Dornier Do 17 Z showing fighter damage, especially on the port wing.

Opposite: This Dornier Do 17 Z, Werk Nummer 2792 of 2/KG 76, was possibly damaged by Flight Lieutenant Archibald Hope and Flying Officer Peter Cleaver of 601 (County of London) Squadron some twelve miles east of Arras, after which it crash-landed at Saint-Ghislain, near Mons in Belgium, at 06.30 hours on 18 May 1940. Oberfeldwebel Rudolf Richter (Flugzeugführer), Oberfeldwebel Willi Laurer (Beobachter), Gefreiter Johannes Buchholz (Bordfunker) and Oberfeldwebel Josef Huber (Bordmechaniker) were all captured. Note the Werk Nummer just visible on the tail, and, in the distance, the spoil heaps which can still be seen around Mons.

The code 5F+PM on the fuselage of this crashed Dornier Do 17 P suggest it was operated by 4(F)/14. It could be the aircraft shot down by Captain Germain Coutaud, Sergeant Coader, Sergeant Roger Teillet and Corporal Josef Pipa of GC I/1, north-east of Chimay, Belgium, on 15 May 1940. It crashed into woods near Givet, France, at 10.10 hours. The Bordmechaniker, Oberfeldwebel Otto Führer, was captured wounded, whilst Oberleutnant Gerhard von Szymonski (Beobachter) and Feldwebel Arnold Sommerla (Flugzeugführer) were both captured unhurt and later released. Alternatively, it could be the Do 17 P shot down on 19 May 1940 by Sergeant Josef Stehlik of GC III/3 during a reconnaissance sortie and crashed on the edge of the Forêt de Mormal near Hachette, south of Locquignol, at 18.20 hours. Leutnant Georg Losse (Flugzeugführer), Unteroffizier Heinrich Ambrosch (Bordfunker) and Leutnant Franz-Josef Menge (Beobachter) were all killed.

This Dornier Do 17 P, coded 4U+CK of 2(F)/123, is believed to have been damaged by Flying Officer Don Cobden of 74 Squadron near Saint-Omer, in northern France, at 10.25 hours on 24 May 1940, with Oberfeldwebel Otto Karg and Feldwebel Heinz Behrens being wounded. Just visible on the nose is the 2(F)/123 badge of a white eagle carrying a telescope on a red and yellow quartered shield.

Badly damaged by flak during a low-level attack at Avesnes, northern France, and possibly crippled by Morane fighters of GC III/2, this Dornier Do 17 Z of 9/KG 76 ended up crashing on the railway line at Beaumont at 12.30 hours on 16 May 1940. Unteroffizier Gotthold Elterich (Beobachter) had been wounded by gunfire and later died in a hospital at Bonn-Venusberg.

An unusual loss on 20 May 1940 was this aircraft, coded Z5+BH, of Aufklärungsstaffel I Flakkorps. Reportedly a Dornier Do 17 M, it was shot down by flak near Reims with Unteroffizier Edgar Berthold (Flugzeugführer) and Leutnant Engel (Beobachter) being captured.

Opposite: This series of images of a badly-damaged Dornier Do 17 Z of 5/KG 76, that coded F1+HN, was taken at Vogelsang airfield in Germany. Initially thought to have been caused on 17 May 1940, when Unteroffizier Otto Stephani was attacking an ammunition dump in the Lens/Arras area, the extensive damage seen here is now believed to have occurred near Saint Omer on 22 May 1940, as it was on this date that Stephani suffered light wounds. Stephani was in hospital for four weeks and was wounded again on 18 August the same year. His Beobachter on 22 May 1940 was Oberleutnant Heinrich Oldendorf, who would be reported missing, whilst Staffelkapitän of 8/KG 76, in April 1943. Note the badge on the nose, which is three yellow arrows on a red and white shield; this emblem was seen on 9/KG 76 aircraft after II/KG 76 disbanded in July 1940.

An unidentified Dornier Do 17 Z having just crash-landed near Arras some time during May 1940.

A Dornier Do 17 Z of Stab/KG 2. This Staffel suffered heavy losses in the Battle of Britain, despite only being between four and six aircraft in strength.

What has happened to cause this much interest is unknown but it would appear that this Dornier Do 17 P has landed on or close to the front line.

This Dornier Do 17 Z, F1+FM of 4/KG 76, was flown by Leutnant Erwin Moll. It was damaged by an RAF fighter, probably that piloted by Flight Lieutenant Terry Webster of 41 Squadron, during a Luftwaffe attack on Dunkirk on 1 June 1940. Such was the damage to his bomber, Moll crash-landed at Haeghe-Meulen, between Ypres and Dunkirk. Moll and Feldwebel Ernst Mössner (Beobachter) were injured, whilst Unteroffizier Hans Fortmüller (Bordfunker) and Unteroffizier Johann Wörlein (Bordmechaniker) were both killed. Having flown with 3/KG 76 in the Battle of Britain, Moll was shot down and taken prisoner on 16 April 1941. The 4 Staffel badge of Great Britain with a bomb landing on it was used by 3/KG 76 after II Gruppe had disbanded pending conversion to the Junkers Ju 88 in July 1941.

Above, left and right: The remains of F1+FM, clearly showing the distinctive badge. (Via Peter Cornwell)

Above: Another view of the distinctive 4/KG 76 badge on F1+JM.

Below: A group of Dornier Do 17 Ps sporting a mix of camouflage schemes. The nearest aircraft still carries its factory codes, whilst the middle aircraft carries the code 4N+TL, showing it to be of 3(F)/22.

This page: On 5 June 1940, 4N+TL of 3(F)/22 was intercepted over Reims by Squadron Leader James More and Flight Officer Edgar 'Cobber' Kain of 73 Squadron. After it force-landed, 4N+TL was destroyed by its crew – Leutnant Wilhelm Telge (Flugzeugführer), Fahnenjunker Walter Rössler and Obergefreiter Heinz Heim, all of whom were captured. Telge became a night fighter pilot but was killed on 1 September 1943. The Staffelkapitän of 5/NJG 1 at the time, he collided with what was believed to be his fourteenth kill.

This aircraft, also from 3(F)/22, has returned with fourteen bullet holes caused by Allied fighters; the date and details are unknown.

Another unidentified 3(F)/22 Dornier Do 17 P. Note again the camouflage, which seems to be common to most of this unit's Battle of France aircraft.

Above and below: The wreckage of another unidentified Dornier Do 17 P. The presence of a medic might indicate that this crash has recently occurred.

Right: The code 5K+LT shows this to be a Dornier Do 17 Z of 9/KG 3. Note the MG 17 ammunition drum in the foreground.

Below: An unidentified wreckage of a Dornier Do 17. In the background is the charred fuselage and in front of that is the wing. Note the grave of one of its crew marked by flowers in the top right-hand corner of the photograph.

All covered up, it is not possible to identify this Dornier Do 17 P's unit.

The holes in the wing of this Dornier Do 17 P are the results of a fighter attack. Note the rear-facing mirror above the cockpit.

The burnt-out wreckage of a Dornier Do 17 that crashed at Langemarck, near Ypres in Belgium. The aircraft's identity has not been established.

German soldiers passing the disintegrated wreckage of a Dornier Do 17 Z.

Above and below: A puzzling scene. In the background is a French Hotchkiss H39 light tank. The two Dornier Do 17 Zs are from KG 76; one has the individual code L, the other K, and both have the fuselage band associated with KG 76 and the code F1+.

Above and opposite: This aircraft is believed to be a Dornier Do 17 Z of 6/KG 76 which was shot down by flak north of Lens at 10.30 hours on 22 May 1940. Oberleutnant Günther Beyer (Flugzeugführer) and Unteroffizier Walter Nikuth (Bordmechaniker) were both captured wounded, whilst Oberleutnant Walter Fundinger (Beobachter) and Obergefreiter Gustav Fischer (Bordfunker) were captured unhurt. All four were later released.

Above: A very new-looking Dornier Do 17 Z, probably from 2./KG 77 as the bat riding a bomb badge is just visible on the nose.

Right and opposite: A Dornier Do 17 Z of 3/KG 76, F1+EL was damaged by Lieutenant Morin of GC III/3 near Mantes-la-Jolie and then crash-landed at Auxile-Château. Leutnant Joachim Hübner (Flugzeugführer) later died of his wounds. Note the last two digits of the Werk Nummer on the nose and the KG 76 fuselage band.

Above and opposite: This Dornier Do 17 Z of 8/KG 2 collided with a Junkers Ju 52 whilst taking off from Kirchberg on 7 June 1940. Amazingly, there were no fatalities, though Hauptmann Joachim Willigmann (Flugzeugführer), Feldwebel Otto Hartge (Flugzeugführer), Oberleutnant Ingo Hollweck-Weithmann (Beobachter), Oberfeldwebel Karl Gross (Bordfunker) and Unteroffizier August Witte (Bordmechaniker) were all injured.

Above, below and opposite: Despite the fact that this crashed Do 17 was frequently photographed by passing German soldiers, the lack of any nose or fuselage bands, or unit emblems, has meant that it has not been possible to establish its identity.

Above: This Dornier Do 17 P was photographed in September 1940. Other photographs of the same wreckage indicate it might be from 1(F)/11, and that the picture was taken at Cerny-lès-Bucy in Northern France.

Below and opposite: A popular subject that was photographed by German soldiers, this was the Dornier Do 17 P coded 6M+BL of 3(F)/11. Some records have this aircraft crash-landing at Aizecourt in Northern France on 29 May 1940. Note that the camouflage is now much darker than seen in aircraft from 3(F)/22 earlier in the Battle of France.

Although from the right period for this section of the book, this crash-landing cannot be identified. The fact that both engines seem to have been working when it crash-landed could indicate it was a training accident.

The numerals 07 on the nose of this Do 17 may indicate that it was Werk Nummer 4107, coded 5F+LM, of 4(F)/14. Having been badly damaged by fighters during a reconnaissance sortie over Douai, 5F+LM made a belly-landing not far from Braibant in Belgium at 07.12 hours on 18 May 1940. Oberleutnant Kurt Heinze, Unteroffizier Rudolf Wagner and Oberfeldwebel Herbert Wetzel were all uninjured.

An unidentified crew of 3(F)/123. This unit was actively involved in the Battle of France and Battle of Britain before converting to the Junkers Ju 88.

German soldiers inspecting a crash-landed and abandoned Dornier Do 17 P; there are no clues as to its unit.

Below and opposite: A Dornier Do 17 P of 2(F)/11 with its rarely seen emblem of a diving eagle. Again, it has not been possible to date the crash.

Another crashed Do 17 being inspected by German soldiers. There are no markings to give a clue as to its unit, but by the look of the path worn around the aircraft, it has been a popular site to visit for some time.

The diagonal noseband indicates that this Dornier Do 17 Z was from KG 2. Though it was photographed in June 1940, a month in which this unit suffered few losses, it has not been possible to make a positive identification.

Photographed in France in July 1940, 5K+HS came from 8/KG 3.

Another unusual loss, this Dornier Do 17 P, coded B4+BA, was from Aufklärungsstaffel Luftflotte 2. It is reported as having crash-landed on the coast between Calais and Nieuport.

Damaged by flak near Metz in north-east France on 19 May 1940, this Dornier Do 17 Z, Werk Nummer 2581, coded U5+DA of Stab/KG 2, succeeded in getting back to crash-land on the western bank of the Saar, near Rehlingen in Germany. There were no crew casualties.

Part IV
THE BATTLE OF BRITAIN AND THE BLITZ

Above and overleaf: The first Dornier Do 17 Z to crash in the United Kingdom came down on 3 July 1940. With the Werk Nummer 2642 and coded 3Z+GS, this aircraft of 8/KG 77 was intercepted by Pilot Officer Peter Gardner, Sergeant William Higgins and Sergeant Edward Bayley of 32 Squadron over Tonbridge in Kent, after which it crashed into a hop field at Paddock Wood at 17.05 hours. Unteroffizier Richard Brandes (Flugzeugführer) and Oberleutnant Hans-Georg Gallion (Beobachter) were both captured wounded; Obergefreiter Erich Hofman (Bordfunker) and Unteroffizier Waldemar Theilig (Bordmechaniker) were both killed. Note the distinctive KG 77 badge, the banner above which reads 'Ich will dasz si vorfechten' (I want them to open the fight). In medieval times, the people of Swabia had the privilege, enshrined in law, that they were to precede the army in any expedition of a German king and allowed to open the battle. Therefore, the Empire Assault Banner, or Reichssturmfahne, was given to them, and was the badge adopted by KG 77.

Another early Battle of Britain casualty was this Dornier Do 17 Z of 2/KG 2. Damaged by fighters during an attack on a convoy off Dover on 10 July 1940, Leutnant Heinz Ermecke (Flugzeugführer) crash-landed back in France with a dead Beobachter, Feldwebel Rudolf Schmidt. It was this crew's first operational flight. In this picture, Ermecke can be seen standing nearest to the camera, whilst in front of him is his believed to be Unteroffizier Götz-Dieter Wolf. Ermecke and Wolf were shot down again on 21 August 1940, by three Hurricanes of 242 Squadron, crashing at Starston in Norfolk. Wolf and two other crew were captured, whilst Ermecke was killed.

Opposite above: This Dornier Do 17 Z of II/KG 3 appears to have returned to France damaged. Note the flat tyre and what appears to be smoke or oxygen coming from the gondola. The aircraft sports the II/KG 3 blackbird badge.

Opposite below: A better view of the II/KG 3 badge, with the 5/KG 3 badge on the cowling.

Early in the morning of 11 July 1940, this Dornier Do 17 Z of 4/KG 2, Werk Nummer 2542 and coded U5+GM, was intercepted off Harwich by the Hurricane of 85 Squadron flown by Squadron Leader Peter Townsend. In the subsequent combat, the Hurricane was shot down and Townsend rescued; the Do 17 limped back to crash-land at Mory, France. Oberleutnant Joachim Genzow (Flugzeugführer) was unwounded, but Leutnant Walter Bornschein (Beobachter), Oberfeldwebel Werner Borner (Bordfunker) and Feldwebel Friedrich Lohrer (Bordmechaniker) were all wounded. The crew members were decorated later in the war – Genzow and Bornschein both being awarded the Ritterkreuz (the latter being killed in action 27 April 1944), and Borner and Lohrer the Deutsches Kreuz in Gold.

Above: Believed to be Hauptmann Reinhard Liebe-Piderit, Staffelkapitän of 3(F)/123, in front of a Dornier Do 17 P. After leading his Staffel successfully in Poland and the Battle of France, on 19 July 1940, he was killed at Buc, north central France, when a captured French aircraft he was flying crashed. Gefreiter Edmund Thiel was also injured in the crash.

Below, opposite and overleaf: What appears to be flak and fighter damage to a Dornier Do 17 P of 3(F)/123. It is possible that this occurred on 10 July 1940, and resulted in the death of Oberleutnant Otto Somborn.

The code 3Z+ identifies this aircraft as being from KG 77. However, despite the letter A being visible, the Staffel letter cannot be seen. KG 77 began converting to the Junkers Ju 88 during the Battle of Britain so Dornier Do 17 losses by this unit are few and far between.

With two flat main wheels and a man pointing out what could be a bullet hole, this unidentified Dornier Do 17 shows clearly the housing for the bomb sight.

Coded U5+AH, this Dornier Do 17 Z of 1/KG 2 was damaged by RAF fighters over the Channel on 10 July 1940 and crash-landed near Wimereux. Obergefreiter Georg Kröhl (Flugzeugführer) and Gefreiter Martin Assum (Bordfunker) were wounded, Feldwebel Franz Enderle (Bordmechanikar) was killed, whilst Oberfeldwebel Karl Deckarm (Beobachter) was uninjured.

Two army personnel posing in front of a Dornier Do 17 in a revetment at Merville, northern France. Merville was the home of I/KG 2 from 8 to 28 March 1941 and II/KG 2 from 17 November 1940 to 28 March 1941.

There are at least ten Dornier Do 17s in this packed hangar. The code 3Z+ can be seen on one aircraft, whilst the one nearest the camera has +FT, which would indicate 9/KG 77. From January 1940, III/KG 77 was commanded by Major Max Kless, who would be killed in action on 18 September 1940, by which time III Gruppe, based at Laon, northern France, was flying the Junkers Ju 88.

Seen in a former French air force hangar is this Dornier Do 17 P with the last two numbers of its Werk Nummer on the nose. In the background is a Junkers Ju 87 of StG 2 (coded T6+L?). However, the badge cannot be discerned.

Recorded as being a Dornier Do 17 M, as opposed to a P variant, of 4(F)/14, this aircraft, coded 5F+OM, was shot down by Squadron Leader Harold Fenton, Flight Lieutenant Don Turner, Pilot Officer John Wigglesworth and Pilot Officer Charles Davis of 238 Squadron. It crash-landed at Blandford in Dorset at 14.45 hours on 21 July 1940. Leutnant Georg Thiel (Beobachter), Feldwebel Fritz Bohnen (Flugzeugführer) and Unteroffizier Alfred Werner (Bordfunker) were all captured wounded.

Two views of the caveman badge which, originally thought to have been used by IV(Erg)/KG 3, is believed to represent I/KG 3. The caveman carried a bomb under his left arm and a trident in his right; the background was apparently blue. This artwork was recorded on a Dornier Do 17 Z-2, Werk Nummer 2544 and coded 5K+CH, of 1/KG 3 which crashed at Boughton Malherbe, Kent, on 28 October 1940.

Though its wreckage is badly disrupted, leaving little to see, this is all that was left of a Dornier Do 17 Z of 2/KG 76, that coded F1+AK, which crashed after take-off at Noailles, Northern France, at 15.30 hours on 30 July 1940. Unteroffizier Hans Schmid (Flugzeugführer), Obergefreiter Rudolf von Kaler (Beobachter), Feldwebel Adolf Diesner (Bordfunker) and Unteroffizier Josef Punger (Bordmechaniker) were all killed. Initially buried at the crash site, they now lie in a cemetery at Beauvais.

Based at Buc on the outskirts of Paris at the time this picture was taken, it was safe for this Dornier Do 17 P, coded 4U+HL of 3(F)/123, to fly over Paris. Note the darkened, as opposed to lighter, camouflage favoured earlier in 1940.

Many Stuka units used aircraft for pre-and post-attack analysis. This Dornier Do 17 P carries the code T6 of StG 2 (presumably T6+FA), which was based at Saint-Malo in Brittany for the Battle of Britain.

Despite the camouflage netting, this is a Dornier Do 17 Z of 2/KG 3 – with code 5K ahead of the cross and last letter is K. Note eight 50kg bombs under the wing ready for loading. I/KG 3 was based at Le Culot, Belgium, during the Battle of Britain.

A similar 'waiting for action' photograph, this time of a Dornier Do 17 Z of KG 76 (code F1 and white L). No Staffel badge is visible, but the full code is either F1+LH (1/KG 76) or F1+LR (7/KG 76). During the Battle of Britain 4/KG 76 converted to the Junkers Ju 88. The base for the former Staffel was Beauvais; the latter was at Cormeilles-en-Vexin.

This aircraft is clearly of KG 2 because of the noseband: if it is red, this is II/KG 2, the colour apparently being applied to the spinners, which would indicate 5/KG 2. The badge is not clear but if it is of 5 Staffel, it is a diving profile of a Dornier superimposed on a globe. Alternatively, it could be the 4/KG 2 bomber with a Middle Eastern man holding a telescope sitting on a bomb. However, this badge has also been recorded on a Dornier Do 17 ZA of Stab/KG 2.

An unidentified, apparently war-weary Dornier Do 17 Z showing clearly the forward defensive armament.

Closer examination of this Do 17 reveals a badge on the nose, which appears to be a shield with three bars on it. This is probably the emblem of 8/KG 76 – a red shield with a black vertical pointing bomb superimposed with the silhouettes of three Dornier Do 17s. This unit was based at Cormeilles-en-Vexin during the Battle of Britain.

This aircraft, coded U5+FH, is a Dornier Do 17 Z of Oberleutnant Karl Kessel's 1/KG 2. On 19 September 1940, Kessel moved to take command of 10/KG 2 and was replaced by Hauptmann Hans-Uwe Ortmann. There is no record of an aircraft carrying this code during 1940, but this could be due to incomplete loss recording. This photograph is possibly taken at Cambrai-Épinoy, northern France.

The badge and red spinners confirm that this Dornier Do 17 is from 2/KG 76. To the right is Oberleutnant Rudolf Hallensleben, who took command of 2 Staffel sometime in August 1940. He would be awarded the Ehrenpokal, Deutsches Kreuz in Gold and Ritterkreuz, and was killed on 19 April 1945 when his vehicle was strafed by American fighters.

Here is the same 2/KG 76 badge seen over the UK in the summer of 1940. It is believed that this badge was discontinued from 1941 onwards.

As nighttime operations over the UK increased, aircraft had to be camouflaged accordingly. This Dornier Do 17 Z from KG 2 has had its noseband toned down and the camouflage darkened.

This is believed to be a Dornier Do 17 Z of 1(F)/122. This unit was based at Lille-Vendeville in Northern France during the Battle of Britain.

Note the unusual device underneath the nose. This Dornier Do 17 Z served with a Wettererkundungsstaffel (Wekusta or Westa), a weather reconnaissance unit.

This Dornier Do 17 Z also has another tube-like device associated with Wekusta aircraft underneath the nose.

Opposite above: Heading for England is a Dornier Do 17 Z, coded U5+AB, of Stab I/KG 76. This aircraft would normally be flown by the Gruppenkommandeur, believed to have been Hauptmann Alois Lindmayr.

Opposite below: U5+IH of 1/KG 2 flies low over what is believed to be Épinoy airfield. Again, this code cannot be linked with a specific aircraft.

An unusually angled photograph of a 2/KG 2 (white noseband, red spinners) Dornier Do 17, which was commanded by Oberleutnant Helmut Powolny during the Battle of Britain.

The upright dragon emblem on this aircraft, also seen on a Junkers Ju 88, suggests that the unit is 7/KG 76, which was based at Cormeilles-en-Vexin shortly before converting to the Ju 88. Note the hastily applied night camouflage.

The aircraft of 9/KG 76 sported a series of badges – this image shows a French cockerel being bombed under the Eiffel Tower. Later, the former badge of 5/KG 76 (three yellow arrows on a red and white shield) was adopted, which was then followed by a wasp.

As the Battle of Britain progressed, armament increased. This Dornier Do 17 Z has a 20mm cannon fitted. Note the crew door, which has written on it 'Go back (*Zurück*) around the engines and enter from the back.'

The view from the Bordfunker's position on a Dornier Do 17.

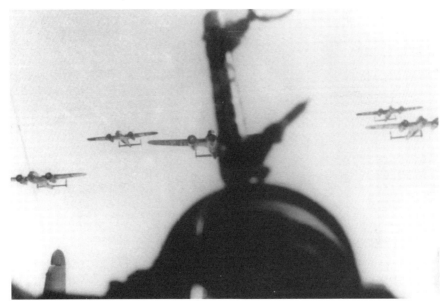

This unidentified Dornier Do 17 Z photographed at Buc has suffered a starboard undercarriage collapse.

Below and opposite: Many photographs of this crash exist, but those reproduced here have recently been discovered in the United States. They show the remains of a Dornier Do 17 Z, that coded U5+DS, of 8/KG 2 which was shot down on to the mudflats at Seasalter in Kent at 07.25 hours on 13 August 1940. Oberleutnant Gerhard Müller (Flugzeugführer), Oberleutnant Werner Morich (Beobachter) and Oberfeldwebel Karl Langner (Bordfunker) were all killed, whilst Feldwebel Rudolf Haensgen (Bordmechaniker) baled out and was captured badly wounded. Both Müller and Morich were initially buried as unknown airmen, their bodies subsequently identified, Morich soon after the war, Müller more recently.

The precise location in the Pas-de-Calais from which Dornier Do 17 Ps of Aufklärungsgruppe 10 (identified in this photograph from the cross in a white shield) operated can be confirmed by what was written on the reverse of this photo – 'St Inglevert'.

Another loss on 13 August 1940, was this Dornier Do 17 Z of Stab/KG 2. Coded U5+KA, it crashed on the railway line at Barham in Kent. Oberleutnant Heinz Schlegel (Flugzeugführer), Oberleutnant Gerhard Osswald (Beobachter and Staffelkapitän), Oberfeldwebel Ernst Holz (Bordfunker) and Oberfeldwebel Gustav Babbe (Bordmechaniker) were all captured, though suffering from varying degrees of injury.

Above and previous page: A remarkable set of images showing the approach of aircraft of 9/KG 76 to the British coast on 18 August 1940. In the last photograph is the Do 17 Z flown by Unteroffizier Günther Unger, whose aircraft was damaged by fighters and ditched a few miles off the French coast on the return flight. The loss of this aircraft resulted in the death of Unteroffizier Karl Moritz (Bordmechaniker). Unger was shot down by flak and captured on the night of 12 March 1941.

The burnt-out remains of Oberleutnant Rudolf Lamberty's Dornier Do 17 Z-2 of 9/KG 76, coded F1+DT, pictured at Leaves Green, Kent, after being shot down whilst attacking Kenley on 18 August 1940. Lamberty, Hauptmann Joachim Roth (Beobachter and Staffelkapitän), Hauptmann Gustav Peters, Feldwebel Hugo Eberhard (Bordfunker) and Oberfeldwebel Valentin Geier (Bordmechaniker) were all captured suffering varying degrees of injuries. The aircraft was reported to have a yellow band around the fuselage and yellow spinners.

Above and below: One of the aircraft that got back on 18 August 1940. This Dornier Do 17 Z-3, F1+CT of 9/KG 76, was flown by Feldwebel Reichel, who managed to crash-land near Abbeville with Unteroffizier Albert Haas (Bordmechaniker) slightly wounded. Reichel, Sonderführer Rolf Von Pebal and one other were uninjured. Note the old 5/KG 76 badge on the nose.

Following damage received whilst attacking Hornchurch on 26 August 1940, this Dornier Do 17 Z-3, with the Werk Nummer 2425 and coded U5+GK, belly-landed two miles south-west of Eastchurch in Kent. Unteroffizier Ambrosius Schmelzer (Flugzeugführer), Major Martin Gutzmann (Beobachter and Gruppenkommandeur) and Unteroffizier Helmut Buhr (Bordfunker) were captured, whilst Oberleutnant Siegfried Hertel (Beobachter) was killed. Gutzmann had been wounded in action on 10 May 1940 and had only recently returned to operational flying.

Another Dornier down in England. This Do 17 Z-4 of 2/KG 76, Werk Nummer 3316 and coded F1+BK, was damaged by flak and probably finished off by Sergeant Maurice Pocock of 72 Squadron. It crash-landed at Newchurch, East Sussex, at 18.00 hours on 31 August 1940. Leutnant Josef Kleppmeier (Flugzeugführer), Oberfeldwebel Heinrich Lang (Beobachter), Feldwebel Harald Pfaehler (Bordfunker) and Unteroffizier Albert Bloss (Bordmechaniker) were all captured. RAF Intelligence reported that the aircraft carried the usual 2/KG 76 badge of a lion being bombed.

This 9/KG 2 Dornier Do 17 Z, coded U5+HT, was forced to land at Coquelles in the Pas-de-Calais sometime in the summer of 1940. The only dates that could match were 11 August 1940, when three 9/KG 2 Do 17s suffered minor damage and wounded crew, and then again on 26 August 1940, when one aircraft was damaged and suffered a wounded Bordfunker. There is no record of a U5+HT in the summer of 1940, although a number of 9/KG 2 aircraft were damaged or lost and their codes not recorded.

Dornier Do 17s over the East End of London. As daylight attacks in greater numbers intensified, it was necessary to paint aircraft with such bars to facilitate air-to-air unit identification.

Above and previous page: This Dornier Do 17 Z-3, which just managed to make it back to France from the late afternoon attack on London on 15 September 1940, was Werk Nummer 2879, coded 5K+AM, of 4/KG 3. With its starboard engine stopped and port engine struggling, Leutnant Sieghard Schopper managed to crash-land on the sand dunes at Mardyck to the east of Calais. Schopper and Staffelkapitän Oberleutnant Bernhard Granicky (Beobachter) were uninjured, whilst Feldwebel Felix Gwidziel (Bordfunker) and Feldwebel Heinz Kirch (Bordmechaniker) were slightly wounded.

Below and opposite: This Dornier Do 17 Z of 8/KG 76, Werk Nummer 2555 and coded F1+FS, was shot down whilst attacking London at 12.10 hours on 15 September 1940. The victors were Flying Officer John Dundas and Pilot Officer Eugene Tobin of 609 (West Riding) Squadron. Feldwebel Rolf Heitsch (Flugzeugführer), Feldwebel Hans Pfeiffer (Bordfunker) and Feldwebel Martin Sauter (Bordmechaniker) were all captured, whilst Feldwebel Stephan Schmid (Beobachter) was mortally wounded. The aircraft was described as having the second 'F' outlined in white, a red band around the fuselage, red spinners and a horizontal pink band on the outside of the rudders. The 8/KG 76 emblem of three white bombers on a red bomb and black shield was on the nose.

Left and opposite: This Dornier Do 17 Z of 2/KG 76, Werk Nummer 2524 and coded F1+JK, was flown by Unteroffizier Hans Figge. His crippled Do 17 managed to get as far as five miles north of Poix, north-eastern France, on 15 September 1940. With one engine stopped due to a fighter attack, Figge successfully crash-landed and the crew clambered out. Oberleutnant Martin Florian (Beobachter) was slightly wounded, whilst Unteroffizier Wagner (Bordfunker) and Ogefr Sommer (Bordmechaniker) were uninjured.

Above and below: Unteroffizier Hans Figge was to crash-land again just nine days later. This is believed to be his aircraft, Dornier Do 17 Z, Werk Nummer 3317 and coded F1+GK, near Boulogne on 24 September 1940. Intercepted by Flying Officer Ian Muirhead and Flying Officer Witold Glowacki of 605 (County of Warwick) Squadron, he force-landed with Unteroffizier Gottfried Curth (Bordmechaniker) slightly wounded. Immediately afterwards, the Hurricanes were attacked by German fighters and Glowacki was shot down, wounded, and captured. He died shortly after from complications.

Photographed at Beauvais just before taking off for London on 15 September 1940, are Feldwebel Karl Niebler (Flugzeugführer), Oberleutnant Karl-Ernst Wilke (Beobachter), Feldwebel Karl Wissmann (Bordschütz), an unknown mechanic, Unteroffizier Hans Schaatz, and Feldwebel Hans Zrenner of 3/KG 76. Behind them is believed to be the Dornier Do 17 Z-3 with the Werk Nummer 2651 and coded F1+FL. Just over an hour later, Wilke and Zrenner would be prisoners of war and the remaining crew dead. Their aircraft crashed and burnt out at Sturry in Kent.

Another aircraft that just got back to Beauvais on 15 September 1940 – F1+EK of 2/KG 76 – with the crew of Unteroffizier Theo Rehm (Beobachter), Feldwebel Ernst Kelmann (Bordmechaniker), Unteroffizier Hans-Joachim Hanke (Flugzeugführer) and Feldwebel Schulz (Bordfunker).

The bulges on the nose of this Dornier Do 17 Z are flotation devices fitted on aircraft predominantly used on maritime attack missions. Designated the Do 17 Z-5, this variant was used almost entirely by Küstenfliegergruppe 606, which operated both maritime and night bombing raids from Lannion and Brest in Western France.

Opposite above: After the failure of daylight attacks, the requirement was for more nighttime attacks. Here temporary black paint is applied to a KG 76 Dornier Do 17. Note the letter F (F1+) and the KG 76 fuselage band.

Opposite below: Another unidentified crash-landing proves interesting to aircrew and ground crew alike.

Above and opposite: The bulges that can be seen in these photographs provide evidence that the aircraft are all Dornier Do 17 Z-5s, almost definitely from Küstenfliegergruppe 606. The last one shows the heavy night camouflage adopted by this unit towards the end of 1940. Küstenfliegergruppe 606 started converting to the Junkers Ju 88 in early 1941.

Above and opposite: Misidentified as a Dornier Do 17 Z-3, this is in fact a Z-5 variant of 1/606, and more specifically that with the Werk Nummer 2787. Coded 7T+HH, it was attacked by Spitfires of 611 (West Lancashire) Squadron while attacking Liverpool on 12 October 1940. It was probably damaged by Flight Lieutenant Bill Leather. With two engines on fire, two of the bomber's crew baled out near Capel Curig in Wales. Feldwebel Willi Staas (Bordfunker) and Unteroffizier Heinz Johannsen (Bordmechaniker) baled out, but the latter is thought to have hit the tail as he was found dead at Deiniolen, seven miles east of Caernarvon, with an unopened parachute. Hans Staas landed at 'Marthalyn' (believed to be Mart of Llyn) and was quickly captured. It was believed that their Do 17 had crashed 'somewhere in the wilds of North Wales' and the remaining two crew members, Oberfeldwebel Willi Hagen (Flugzeugführer) and Oberleutnant zS Karl-Franz Heine (Beobachter), were missing. However, Hagen managed to get his crippled Do 17 back to France and landed at Brest. The bomber shows many signs of the combat with 611 Squadron and, sadly, where Heinz Johannsen had probably hit the tail. Willi Hagen, who would be decorated with the Deutsches Kreuz in Gold and Ehrenpokal, was killed over Malta on 19 April 1942. Karl-Franz Heine returned to serve on U-boats and would be killed on 18 August 1943 commanding *U-403*, which was sunk south-west of Dakar by a Lockheed Hudson of 200 Squadron and a Wellington of 697 Squadron.

Difficult to see as it is blacked out, this Dornier Do 17 Z of 9/KG 3 (5K and the last letter T are just visible) has crash-landed, presumably at St Trond in Belgium. Its unit badge has also been blacked out.

Although its markings have been blacked out, the noseband has not, which clearly identifies this as a KG 2 aircraft. The officer to the left speaking to two Italian and one German officers is Major Klaus Uebe, who took command of III/KG 2 on 1 September 1940 when his predecessor, Major Adolf Fuchs, was wounded. Uebe handed over to Major Friedrich Dreyer on 20 March 1941. During this time, III/KG 2 was based at Cambrai Süd.

Difficult to identify is this heavily toned-down Dornier Do 17 Z, pictured having crashed somewhere in France or Belgium.

Probably a Dornier Do 17 Z of KG 77, by the time of the Blitz this unit had all but converted to the Junkers Ju 88.

Above: A Dornier Do 17 Z of 5/KG 2 coded U5+AN, which has taxied into a bomb crater at Cambrai Süd on returning from an attack on London on the night of 27 October 1940. The crew were Unteroffizier Ernst Fröhlich (Bordfunker; PoW on 15 May 1944), Leutnant Karl Manowarda (Fliege; also PoW on 15 May 1944), Oberfeldwebel Helmut Petraschke (Beobachter), and Unteroffizier Ernst Geselle (Bordmechaniker; killed 25 June 1942).

Right: One of the last losses of Küstenfliegergruppe 606 before it converted to the Junkers Ju 88. At 20.15 hours on 9 November 1940, Dornier Do 17 Z coded 7T+KH of 1/606, with the Werk Nummer 2683, crashed for unknown reasons into a wood near Liskeard in Cornwall. Oberfeldwebel Walter Seifert (Flugzeugführer), Leutnant zur See Günther Senhorst (Beobachter), Unteroffizier Heinz Winkler (Bordfunker) and Obergefreiter Heinz Hassloff (Bordmechaniker) were all killed. (Via Cornish Studies Library)

Leutnant Hans-Joachim Dutz of 2/606 in front of his Dornier Do 17 Z-5, in late 1940. He would convert to the Junkers Ju 88, only to be killed in action 28/29 May 1941.

Partially camouflaged for night operations, this Dornier Do 17 Z of 1/KG 2 is coded U5+E(or F)H. The fact that most of the men in this picture are wearing overcoats would indicate that this photo was taken after the Battle of Britain and the lack of damage would be under 50 per cent, but there are no likely candidates.

Part V
AFTER THE BLITZ, 1941 AND BEYOND

Sitting in its revetment is what appears to be a Dornier Do 17 Z bomber, though closer examination and the background indicates that this is a Do 17 Z-7 or Z-10 night fighter of 5/NJG 1 (later 2/NJG 2).

Above and below: A Dornier Do 17 Z-10 of 5/NJG 1 equipped with the infra-red (IR) Spanner Anlage illuminator in the nose and the scope in the cockpit. This was an active IR system, and, using IR illumination from the nose, did not rely at all on passive detection of a target's exhaust radiation. It had a maximum range of 650 feet and painted the target aircraft in a red glow; there was no visible light on the attacking aircraft. The popular name for the system was 'Peeping Tom Installation'.

In March 1941, III/KG 3 moved to Austria in preparation for attacks on Yugoslavia. This Dornier Do 17 Z of 8/KG 3 is taxiing out for an attack on Belgrade. The Ace of Clubs has now moved from the nose to the outside of the cowlings.

Aircraft of II/KG 2 photographed at Zwölfaxing in Austria preparing to take off for another attack on Belgrade, Easter 1941.

Opposite: A very popular aircraft to be photographed was this Dornier Do 17 Z, 5K+GT of 9/KG 3, which crash-landed at Kozani in Greece on 16 April 1941 and suffered 30 per cent damage. Although hard to see, the cowlings of this aircraft were painted yellow, which was applied to aircraft for the Greek campaign, as were the rudders of a number of aircraft types.

Another II/KG 2 Dornier Do 17 at an unidentified airfield during the Yugoslavia campaign. Note the red band on the nose and the fact that the aircraft is camouflaged for daylight operations.

A Dornier Do 17 Z, probably from I/KG 2 (white noseband), photographed during the attack on the Soviet Union (the aircraft has a yellow fuselage band). I/KG 2 moved to Göttingen, Germany from Athens-Tatoi on 1 June 1941 and then moved to Arys-Rostken (then in East Prussia, now in Poland) on 18 June 1941. It was based at Suwalki, Silce, Wereteni and Rjelbitzy in the Soviet Union during the summer of 1941.

Opposite above: This Dornier Do 17 P is identified as being from 2(F)/11 by the badge. Werk Nummer 4153 force-landed at Horopani in Bulgaria on 16 April 1941, with 40 per cent damage. Note the cowling colour.

Opposite below: The remains of a Dornier Do 17 Z probably photographed at a Greek airfield during the Greek campaign – the unit, date and cause have not been identified.

The unit that operated this Do 17 cannot be identified. The letter A and the yellow fuselage band, however, indicate that the picture was taken during the summer of 1941.

An engine change and repairs are pictured being carried out on U5+ZT, Werk Nummer 2797, of 9/KG 2. On 4 July 1941, U5+ZT force-landed at Suwalki after returning from an attack on Smolensk, suffering 30 per cent damage. Leutnant Wolfgang Hankamer (Flugzeugführer), Unteroffizier Max Schedel (Beobachter), Gefreiter Wilhelm Tebbe (Bordfunker) and Gefreiter Friedrich Bergau (Bordmechaniker) were all uninjured. This crew was particularly successful, the pilot being awarded the Ritterkreuz, the remainder the Deutsches Kreuz in Gold. Hankamer was killed in action on 14 January 1945, whilst commanding 1/JG 301.

An unidentified Dornier Do 17 Z, believed to be from 1/KG 2, crash-landed during the Russian campaign in the summer of 1941. The white band indicates I/KG 2, and it appears to have the 1/KG 2 eagle carrying a bomb badge on the nose.

Another I/KG 2 crash-landing. The location is Witebsk (Vitebsk, Belarus). Stab and I/KG2 were based at Witebsk from 1 October to 1 November 1941, and the trees in the background would indicate this timescale. Noting the damage, it is possible that this is Werk Nummer 3340 of Stab/KG 2, which was damaged by flak attacking Kalinin and force-landed at Witebsk on 7 October 1941 with 30 per cent damage.

A crew from Stab/KG 2 photographed in the summer of 1941. Left to right are an unknown mechanic; Unteroffizier Willi Schludecker (Flugzeugführer); Leutnant Walter Hosemann (Beobachter); Feldwebel Hein Bühr (Bordmechaniker); and Gefreiter Alfons Bemmelmanns (Bordfunker). All but Hosemann, who would be killed in action on 21 October 1941, would be awarded the Ehrenpokal.

On 8 October 1941, the aircraft flown by Schludecker and his crew was hit by flak. With a burning engine, they force-landed U5+KA near Cholm, Russia, at 07.40 hours. They arrived back at Witebsk, in a Junkers Ju 52, at 16.02 hours the same day. They flew their next mission two days later.

This Do 17 of 7/KG 3 was pictured at Wjasma (Vyasma) in the Soviet Union, where the unit was based in November and December 1941, after when it returned to Germany to convert to the Junkers Ju 88.

Despite the mix of Dornier Do 17 Zs and Heinkel He 111s, where and when this photograph was taken is a puzzle. The He 111 nearest the camera has a fuselage band indicating the Russian Front and the badges on the noses of the Do 17s are different, whilst the furthest Do 17 has a vertical band that bisects four badges.

With the Junkers Ju 88 replacing the Dornier Do 17, most were now assigned secondary roles. The nearest aircraft served on Grosse Kampffliegerschule 1 at Tutow, Germany, and ultimately with Flugzeugführerschule C4. Its ultimate fate is not known.

There were four Aufklärungsstaffel (Nacht), numbered 1 to 4, which operated over the Eastern Front from late 1941 onwards, initially flying Dornier Do 17 M and P but then more modern aircraft. This photograph shows a mix of all black Do 17 Ps and Zs.

There are no less than twenty-four Dornier Do 17 Zs in this photograph taken on the Eastern Front in 1942. It is assumed that the unit that once operated them had converted to the Junkers Ju 88.

This Dornier Do 17 P was photographed carrying out transport duties in Italy in 1943.

On 30 July 1944, this Dornier Do 17 Z-5 of 1/Kampfgruppe Kroatien, with the Werk Nummer 2899 and coded Z8+AH, crash-landed at Cerignola, just south of Foggia in Italy. Having taken off from Lučko in Croatia, whilst en route to Konigsberg in Russia (one of a formation of five Do 17s and four Ju 87s), it turned towards the Adriatic, and its crew, including the pilot, Leutnant Albin Vouk, defected to the Allies.